R0061229837

08/2011

Abe Lincoln
AND THE MUDDY PIG

written by
Stephen Krensky

illustrated by
Gershom Griffith

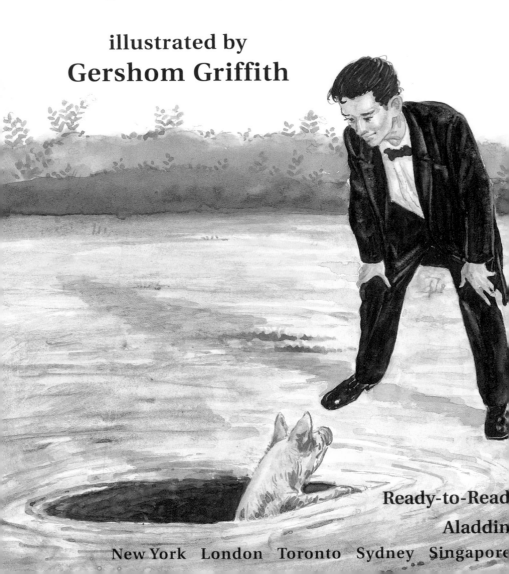

Ready-to-Read

Aladdin

New York   London   Toronto   Sydney   Singapore

For Uncle Joel.
—S.K.

First Aladdin edition January 2002
Text copyright © 2002 by Stephen Krensky
Illustrations copyright © 2002 by Gershom Griffith

Aladdin Paperbacks
An imprint of Simon & Schuster
Children's Publishing Division
1230 Avenue of the Americas
New York, NY 10020

READY-TO-READ is a registered trademark of Simon & Schuster, Inc.
The text for this book was set in 17 Point Utopia
Designed by Lisa Vega
The illustrations were rendered in watercolor

Printed and bound in the United States of America
20 19 18   17 16 15 14 13 12

Library of Congress Cataloging-in-Publication Data
Krensky, Stephen.
Abe Lincoln and the muddy pig / by Stephen Krensky ; illustrated by
Greshom Griffith.—1st Aladdin Paperbacks ed.
p. cm.—(Ready-to-read)
Summary: A young Abe Lincoln stumbles across a pig in trouble and
decides he must help, even though it will mean arriving late and muddy for
the important speech he is scheduled to make.
ISBN 0-689-84112-4
ISBN 0-689-84103-5 (pbk.)
0110 LAK
1. Lincoln, Abraham, 1809–1865—Childhood and youth—Juvenile literature.
2. Presidents—United States—Biography--Juvenile literature. 3. Pigs—
Indiana—Juvenile literature. [1. Lincoln, Abraham, 1809–1865—Childhood
and youth. 2. Presidents. 3. Pigs.] I. Griffith, Greshom, ill. II. Title. III. Series.
E457.32.K74 2002
973.7'092—dc21
[B]
2001046124)

Young Abe Lincoln was in a hurry.
Most of the time his days were filled
with farm chores or odd jobs.
But today was different.
Today, he was going to town
to give a big speech.

2

Abe liked to make speeches.
He hadn't had much schooling,
less than a year altogether,
but he knew lots of stories.
"The things I want to know
are in books," he said.
"My best friend is the man
who'll get me a book I haven't read."
Abe also loved to learn to spell big words
even before he had a use for them.
He just stored them up
like a squirrel saving nuts for winter.

Abe got dressed and
gave his thick hair a brushing.
Then he straightened up to his full
height—six feet four inches
in his stocking feet.
Abe was hard to miss in a crowd.
His father called him
the "awkwardest fellow
that ever stepped over a ten-rail fence."

Abe patted the sleeve of his new suit,
the first one he had ever owned.
Mostly, he wore a homespun shirt
and a pair of buckskin pants
that never quite seemed long enough
to catch up with his ankles.

Abe had paid for the suit by splitting
hundreds of wooden fence rails.
Nobody in the county
could split rails like Abe.
He knew just how high to swing the ax,
and just the right moment
to shift his weight for the final blow.

Abe was handy with lots of tools.
He knew how to hammer and saw,
and how to cut hay.
He could skin the hide of a deer
or butcher a hog into a month of meals.

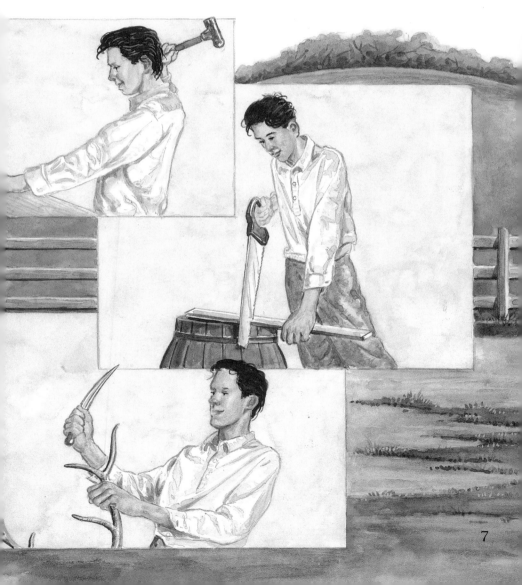

But none of that was on his mind
as he started out for town.
He had his speech to think about.

Abe's long strides
covered the ground quickly.
Five or ten miles was nothing more
than a good stroll to him.
When he lived in Indiana,
he walked nine miles
each way to school.
One day he walked thirty-four miles
just to hear a lawyer give a speech
he was curious about.
Abe hoped his audience today
would be curious about his words, too.

As Abe came over a hill,
he saw a pig rolling in the mud.
The pig was grunting
and snorting up a storm.
At first Abe thought the pig was playing.
"You're having a fine time for yourself,"
he said.
But then he watched more closely.
He realized that the pig was struggling.
"I do believe you're stuck," said Abe.
The pig only snorted
—and wriggled some more.

Now, Abe didn't like to see
any animal suffer.
When he was eight,
he shot and killed a wild turkey
outside his cabin.
Seeing that dead bird had left
a funny feeling in his stomach.
After that, he gave up hunting.
And he always spoke right up
if anyone was cruel to an animal—
even just stepping on an ant.

Of course, nobody was planning
to step on the pig.
And its life wasn't in danger either.
It just looked scared and alone.
"I am sorry, young pig," said Abe.
"But I cannot come to your rescue.
I am wearing my new suit,
and I have to give a speech
in less than an hour."

Abe stepped around the mudhole
and moved on.
He tried to put the pig out of his mind.
His speech was what mattered.
He thought about all the people
who would be coming to listen to him.

"Keep thinking about that speech,"
he told himself.
But it did no good.
His thoughts kept returning
to the poor little pig.

Finally, Abe stopped in his tracks.
A pig might not be a person,
but it still deserved his help.
Abe sighed
and returned to the mudhole.
The pig was still there.

"Easy," said Abe.

"We'll have you out in two shakes."

Now, Abe was a champion wrestler.

Folks reckoned him

maybe the best wrestler

they had ever seen.

But the pig didn't know that.

It didn't realize

Abe was only trying to help.

So it put up a pretty good fight.

By the time Abe freed the pig
from the mud,
it was hard to tell them apart.

Abe looked down at his muddy suit
and shook his head.
But there was no time to go home
and change.
Besides, he didn't have anything better
to wear.

When Abe got to town,
he found a crowd gathering.
In the past he had enjoyed
standing on a tree stump
or a fence to talk to other farmers.
But this was more than just a chat
among friends.

Abe's audience had come
to hear him speak
about their dreams for the future.
They were hoping he could
put into words the feelings and ideas
they couldn't quite say for themselves.

Abe's speech was about the river
and how important it was to their lives.
The river provided water, of course,
and also power to run the grist and
sawmills.

But rivers were also the best way
to move goods.
The country was growing up fast,
Abe explained.
They needed to make traveling by river
safe and secure.
That would help everyone
in the long run.

When Abe spoke, he didn't
shout or make people nervous.
He spoke plainly,
listing his facts one by one
and then weaving them together
to make a point.

His hands followed the pace
of his words, moving in and out
of his pockets as he spoke.
Abe hated when anyone spoke
in a way he couldn't understand.
So he made sure he didn't talk too fancy.

The mud on his suit was still there,
but nobody seemed likely to mention it.
People cared more about what Abe said
than how he looked.

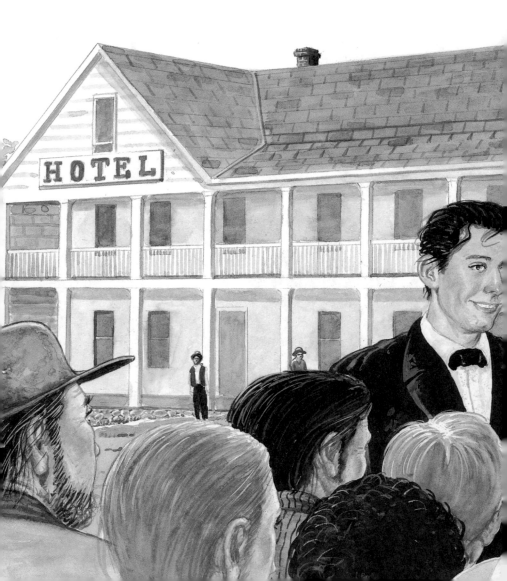

People nodded as he spoke,
and clapped when he was done.
The speech had been a great success.
Why, even the pig seemed to like it.

This book is based on a story passed down about Abraham Lincoln. The timeline below outlines important events in his life.

1809   Born near Hodgenville, Kentucky

1816   Moves to Indiana

1817   Mother dies
Father remarries Sarah Bush Johnson

1818   Family moves to Illinois

1834   Elected to the state legislature
Studies to be a lawyer

1837   Moves to the state capital at Springfield

1842   Marries Mary Todd
Later has four children

1846   Elected to United States Congress

1858   Runs for U.S. Senate, but loses to
Stephen A. Douglas

1860   Elected president of the United States

1861   Civil War begins in April

1863   Issues Emancipation Proclamation,
freeing the slaves
Gives Gettysburg Address, calling for the
country to remain united

1864   Re-elected to a second term

1865   Civil War ends on April 9
Lincoln is assassinated five days later on
April 14 at Ford's Theater